DANIEL AND THE LIONS

Activity Book

To Jack,
Happy First Communion.
May you always know
that Jesus is with
you always!
God Bless,
Aunt Susan
and
Ann Marie.
4/29/2023

Daniel and the Lions Activity Book

Bible Pathway Adventures® is a trademark of BPA Publishing Ltd.
Defenders of the Faith® is a trademark of BPA Publishing Ltd.

ISBN: 978-1-989961-71-1

Author: Pip Reid

Creative Director: Curtis Reid

For free Bible resources including coloring pages, worksheets, puzzles and more, visit our website at:

www.biblepathwayadventures.com

◆◇ INTRODUCTION ◇◆

Enjoy teaching your children about the Bible with our hands-on *Daniel and the Lions Activity Book for Kids Ages 6-12*. Packed with detailed lesson plans, coloring pages, fun worksheets, and puzzles to help educators just like you teach children the Biblical faith. Includes ESV scripture references for easy Bible verse look-up, and a handy answer key for teachers.

Bible Pathway Adventures helps educators teach children about the Biblical faith in a fun and creative way. We do this via our Activity Books, Bible storybooks, and free printable activities – available on our website: www.biblepathwayadventures.com

Thanks for buying this Activity Book and supporting our ministry. Every book purchased helps us continue our work providing free Classroom Packs and discipleship resources to families and missions around the world.

The search for Truth is more fun than Tradition!

★BONUS★

Our illustrated Daniel and the Lions storybook is available for download.
Type the link into your browser to get your free copy today!
https://BookHip.com/JLLQR

◆◇ TABLE OF CONTENTS ◇◆

LESSON 1 | Lesson Plan
The king's dream

Teacher: _____

Today's Bible passage: Daniel 1:1–2:48

Welcome prayer:
Pray a simple prayer with the children before you begin the lesson.

Lesson objectives:
In this lesson, children will learn:
1. The kingdom where Daniel and his friends lived
2. How the king rewarded Daniel for his help

Did You Know?
Babylon was 900 miles away from Jerusalem.

Bible lesson overview:
In the third year of the reign of King Jehoiakim of Judah, King Nebuchadnezzar of Babylon came to Jerusalem and besieged it. He stole gold and silver items from the temple, and took many Hebrews back to Babylon, including Daniel and his friends Shadrach, Meshach, and Abednego. Daniel and his friends lived at the palace and began to work for the king. One night, the king had a dream about a giant statue. The statue was made of gold, silver, bronze, and iron. No one could tell him the meaning of his dream. But God helped Daniel understand the king's dream. The king was pleased with Daniel. He made him ruler over Babylon, and chief governor over all the magi.

Let's Review:

Questions to ask your students:

1. Why did Daniel and his friends move to Babylon?
2. Who did Daniel work for?
3. Read Daniel 2:36-43. What did King Nebuchadnezzar see in his dream?
4. Who helped the king understand his dream?
5. How did the king reward Daniel?

 A memory verse to help children remember God's Word:

"…God gave them learning and skill in all literature and wisdom, and Daniel had understanding in all visions and dreams." (Daniel 1:17)

 ## Activities:

Worksheet: The southern kingdom

Map activity: The Babylonian Empire

Labyrinth: Taken to Babylon

Worksheet: Did You Know?

Bible quiz: Daniel in Babylon

What's the word? Daniel's faithfulness

Bible word search puzzle: The king's dream

Coloring worksheet: The king's dream

Worksheet: I had a dream

Coloring page: The king's dream

Comprehension worksheets: King Nebuchadnezzar

 ## Closing prayer:

End the lesson with a small prayer.

The southern kingdom

When Israel divided after King Solomon's death (926 BC), the Israelites were split into two kingdoms. The southern kingdom was called Judah, and included the tribes of Judah and Benjamin. The northern kingdom was called Israel, and included the tribes of Reuben, Simeon, Manasseh, Issachar, Zebulun, Ephraim, Dan, Asher, Naphtali and Gad. In approximately 586 BC, King Nebuchadnezzar of Babylon attacked Jerusalem. The temple was destroyed, and the tribes of Judah and Benjamin were largely deported to Babylon. Research the tribes of Judah and Benjamin. On the lines below, write the names of famous Bible characters from these two tribes. How many can you name?

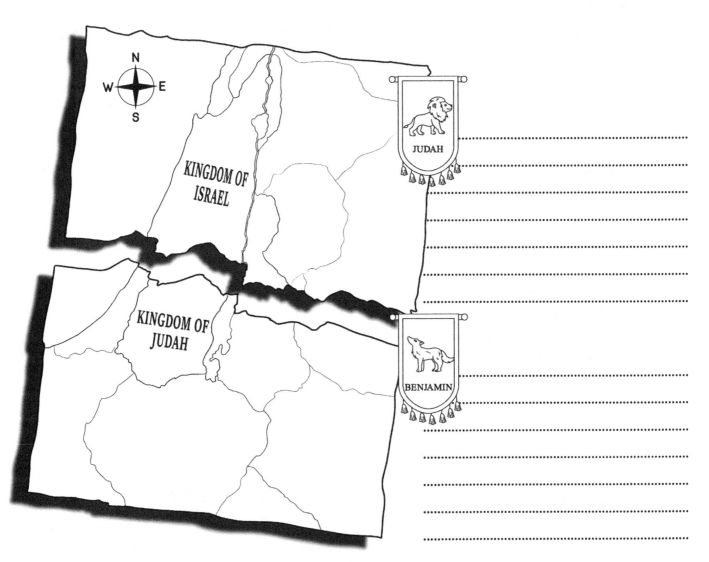

The Babylonian Empire

The Babylonian Empire was the most powerful state in the ancient world after the fall of the Assyrian empire. Even after the Babylonian Empire had been overthrown by the Persian king Cyrus the Great, the city of Babylon remained an important cultural center. Find and mark the boundaries of the Babylonian Empire on the map. Add the places in the map key to the map. You may need to use the Internet or a historical atlas to find the answers.

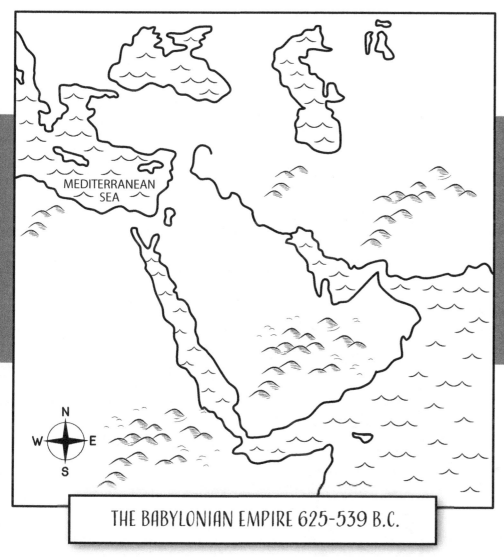

MEDITERRANEAN SEA

N
W   E
S

THE BABYLONIAN EMPIRE 625-539 B.C.

Find and mark these places:

JERUSALEM
TYRE
BABYLON
UR
EGYPT

EUPHRATES RIVER
NINEVEH
SUSA
SYRIA
DAMASCUS

Taken to Babylon

Daniel and his friends were taken to Babylon (Daniel 1:3-4).
Help the Babylonian army return to Babylon with their Hebrew prisoners.

Bible Pathway Adventures

Did you know?

"In the third year of the reign of Jehoiakim king of Judah, King Nebuchadnezzar of Babylon came to Jerusalem and besieged it." (Daniel 1:1) The king conquered Jerusalem, captured some of its royals and noble young men, and took them into captivity in Babylon. In the late 19th century, archaeologists discovered a cuneiform tablet (known as Jehoiachin's Rations Tablet) in the ancient city of Babylon in Iraq. It listed the rations given to 'Ya'u-kīnu, king of the land of Yāhudu,' his five sons, and other royal captives after they were exiled to Babylon. In 2 Kings 25:27-30 and Jeremiah 52:31-34, the Bible records Jehoiachin receiving relatively favorable rations from the Babylonian king, as well as the presence of other royal deportees in Babylon.

Read Daniel 1:1-2. What do you think the siege of Jerusalem looked like? Draw a scene from this Bible passage.

DANIEL IN BABYLON

Read Daniel 1:1-2:48 (ESV).
Answer the questions below.

1. Who did King Nebuchadnezzar command Ashpenaz to bring back to Babylon? ....

2. Name four Israelites who were deported to Babylon. ....

3. What did Daniel resolve to do in Daniel 1:8? ....

4. What did God give Daniel? ....

5. Who could not interpret King Nebuchadnezzar's dream? ....

6. Why did the king want to kill the wise men of Babylon? ....

7. How did God reveal to Daniel the meaning of the king's dream? ....

8. What was Daniel's Babylonian name? ....

9. What was the statue in the king's dream made from? ....

10. How did the king reward Daniel? ....

DANIEL'S FAITHFULNESS

Read Daniel 1:8-20 (ESV). Fill in the blanks below.

"Daniel asked the chief of the eunuchs to allow him not to .... himself. God gave Daniel favor and .... in the sight of the chief. The chief said to Daniel, "I fear the king, who assigned your food and drink; for why should he see that you were in worse condition than the youths who are of your own age? You would .... my head with the king." Daniel said to the steward whom the chief of the eunuchs had assigned over Daniel, Hananiah, Mishael, and Azariah, "Test your .... for ten days; give us vegetables to eat and water to drink. Let our appearance and the appearance of the youths who eat the king's food be observed by you, and deal with your servants according to what you see." He .... to them and tested them for ten days. At the end of .... days it was seen that they were better in .... and fatter in flesh than the youths who ate the king's food. The .... took away their food and the wine they were to drink, and gave them vegetables. As for these four youths, God gave them learning and skill in all literature and wisdom, and Daniel had understanding in all .... and dreams. At the end of the time, when the king had .... they should be brought in, the chief of the eunuchs brought them before Nebuchadnezzar. The .... spoke with them, and among all of them none was found like Daniel, Hananiah, Mishael, and Azariah. In every matter of .... and understanding… he found them ten times better than all the magicians and enchanters in his kingdom."

DEFILE	VISIONS
SERVANTS	COMPASSION
KING	COMMANDED
APPEARANCE	TEN
ENDANGER	LISTENED
WISDOM	STEWARD

THE KING'S DREAM

Read Daniel 2:1-45 (ESV).
Find and circle each of the words from the list below.

```
T L N H K F E U D R E A M O J A
M P D W J N Q J Q V R W E H R T
H R K U I J A A X I Z L V K P C
E B B V Y S J R F S J X I N B P
C L A Y K U E A K I N Z E O R B
I R O N S X L M E O L K P W O A
A C I D P K D A E N C N T L N J
R O S K A D Q I C N X I D E Z P
I L Y D N N X C M C R G K D E G
O E T K Z C I B Y W R A A G A C
C B F B P J E E V X A O J E H G
H U G M Y P K Z L U N B W J O O
I N T E R P R E T A T I O N C L
C H A L D E A N S X S T O N E D
U N E B U C H A D N E Z Z A R T
R E S A W I N S T A T U E R B A
```

INTERPRETATION	NEBUCHADNEZZAR	STONE	KNOWLEDGE
GOLD	ARIOCH	DREAM	STATUE
CHALDEANS	CLAY	ARAMAIC	DANIEL
VISION	IRON	BRONZE	WISEMEN

The king's dream

Read Daniel 2:1 and write the Bible verse below.

....

....

....

1. What did the king dream about?

....

....

2. Describe the statue from King Nebuchadnezzar's dream.

....

....

3. How did God reveal the meaning of the king's dream to Daniel?

....

....

Draw your favorite scene from Daniel 2.

Daniel interpreted the king's dream because...

....

....

Daniel was promoted by the king because...

....

....

I had a dream

Read Daniel 2:31-35. Imagine you are King Nebuchadnezzar.
Explain your dream to Daniel. Color the statue according to the king's description.

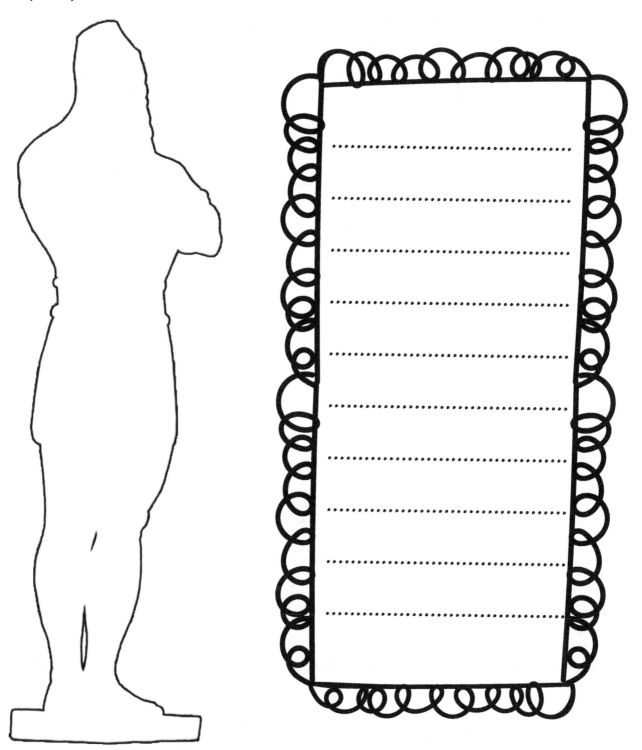

"...Nebuchadnezzar had dreams; his Spirit was troubled, and his Sleep left him."

(Daniel 2:1)

KING NEBUCHADNEZZAR II

This article explains the reign of King Nebuchadnezzar.
Read the text and answer the questions on the next page.

Nebuchadnezzar II was considered the greatest king of the Babylonian Empire. He ruled for 43 years, from approximately 605 BC until approximately 562 BC. During his reign, he completed many building projects including the construction of a double wall ten miles long that surrounded the city of Babylon, and a magnificent entry called the Ishtar Gate. Many scholars believe it was Nebuchadnezzar II who built the Hanging Gardens of Babylon.

Nebuchadnezzar II was most famous for conquering Judah and the destruction of Jerusalem. The Babylonians first attacked and captured Jerusalem in 597 BC, taking King Jehoiachin and his family into exile. But Nebuchadnezzar II was brutal, powerful, and ambitious. When he realized Judah had not learnt its lesson from his first invasion, he returned and destroyed the temple and most of Jerusalem, bringing an end to the southern kingdom of Judah. Hebrew people from both campaigns were taken back to Babylon, including Daniel and his friends. God used Nebuchadnezzar II to judge Judah for its idolatry, unfaithfulness, and disobedience.

"…behold, I will send for all the tribes of the north,' declares the Lord, 'and for Nebuchadnezzar the king of Babylon, my servant, and I will bring them against this land and its inhabitants, and against all these surrounding nations…" (Jeremiah 25:9).

As prophesied in Scripture, the children of Israel were allowed to return to Jerusalem after seventy years in Babylon. This prophecy was fulfilled in 537 BC when King Cyrus of Persia let the children of Israel return to the land of Israel to begin rebuilding the city. Their return led to the rebuilding of the temple in Jerusalem. Both the captivity/exile and the return and restoration of the Israelite nation fulfilled Old Testament prophecies.

Homework

Mission objective: To understand the life of King Nebuchadnezzar.
Read each question and write your answer on the lines below.

How long did King Nebuchadnezzar rule the Babylonian Empire?

....

....

Name some building projects that King Nebuchadnezzar completed during his reign.

....

....

What was King Nebuchadnezzar most famous for?

....

....

Why were the children of Israel allowed to return to Jerusalem?

....

....

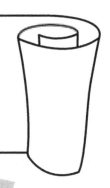

LESSON 2 | Lesson Plan
Handwriting on the wall

Teacher: _____

Today's Bible passage: Daniel 5:1-31

Welcome prayer:
Pray a simple prayer with the children before you begin the lesson.

Lesson objectives:
In this lesson, children will learn:
1. Why God was not pleased with King Belshazzar
2. The meaning of the handwriting on the wall

Did You Know?
The words on the wall were written in an ancient language called Aramaic. This was the language of public life and administration in Babylon.

Bible lesson overview:
King Belshazzar held a feast for a thousand officials at his palace in Babylon. They drank wine using gold and silver vessels stolen from the temple in Jerusalem. But God was not pleased with the king for using the vessels. All of a sudden, the fingers of a human hand wrote strange words on the wall. The king was very afraid! What did the words mean? The king's mother remembered that Daniel, the chief of the Magi, could understand secrets and dreams. Daniel came to the palace and explained the meaning of the words. "Your kingdom is being taken from you," he told Belshazzar. That night, enemy soldiers entered the palace and killed the king, and a man called Darius became the new king.

Let's Review:

Questions to ask your students:

1. Who attended the king's feast?
2. During the feast, what did the king use to drink wine?
3. Was God pleased with the king's behavior? Why/why not?
4. What was the meaning of the words written on the wall?
5. How did the king reward Daniel for helping him understand the handwriting on the wall?

 A memory verse to help children remember God's Word:

"…the fingers of a human hand appeared and wrote on the wall of the king's palace…" (Daniel 5:5)

 Activities:

Bible quiz: Handwriting on the wall

Coloring page: The king's feast

Newspaper worksheet: The king's feast

Worksheet: Temple in Jerusalem

Bible word unscramble: Handwriting on the wall

Bible craft: Writing on the wall

Worksheet: Did you know?

Worksheet: Aramaic alphabet

Worksheet: The king's feast

Worksheets: The Magi

Bible craft: Daniel's gold chain

 Closing prayer:
End the lesson with a small prayer.

HANDWRITING ON THE WALL

Read Daniel 5:1-31 (ESV).
Answer the questions below.

1. Who made a great feast for a thousand of his lords? ....

2. Where were the golden vessels stolen from? ....

3. What wrote on the plaster of the palace wall? ....

4. How did the king react when he saw the handwriting? ....

5. What words were written on the wall? ....

6. Who did the king ask to interpret the handwriting? ....

7. Who did the queen declare could help the king understand the
    handwriting? ....

8. What was the meaning of the handwriting on the wall? ....

9. How did the king reward Daniel? ....

10. Who became king after Belshazzar? ....

"King Belshazzar made a great feast for a thousand of his lords and drank wine" in front of them.

(Daniel 5:1)

City of Babylon

The
Babylonian Times

DANIEL 5 BABYLONIA A BIBLE HISTORY PUBLICATION

Handwriting at palace

....

....

....

....

....

....

New ziggurat!

King hosts party for 1000!

....

....

....

....

www.biblepathwayadventures.com
Daniel and the Lions Activity Book

© BPA Publishing Ltd 2022

24

Temple in Jerusalem

When King Nebuchadnezzar destroyed the city of Jerusalem, his soldiers stole the gold and silver vessels from the temple and took them back to Babylon. King Solomon had built the temple many years prior to the king's invasion (Daniel 5:3). His father David had even stockpiled large amounts of gold, silver, iron, timber and stone for this project. However, God did not allow David to build the temple during his lifetime. "You have been a man of war," He said. "I want a man of peace."

It took Solomon seven years to build the temple in Jerusalem. To do this, he organized a peacetime draft to find enough workers for the job. As many as 30,000 Israelites (divided into three monthly shifts) were sent to work in Phoenicia to cut the timber needed to build the temple. Huge rafts were built to float the logs to the land of Israel via the Mediterranean Sea. Meanwhile, Phoenician craftsmen worked side-by-side with the Israelites at the temple site in Jerusalem. While the temple was the main project, many other buildings were built to support temple activities, including the treasury buildings, granaries, livestock holding pens for sacrifices, and housing for the priests

1. Read I Chronicles 29: What materials did David stockpile to build the temple?

   ....

2. Why do you think it took Solomon seven years to build the temple?

   ....

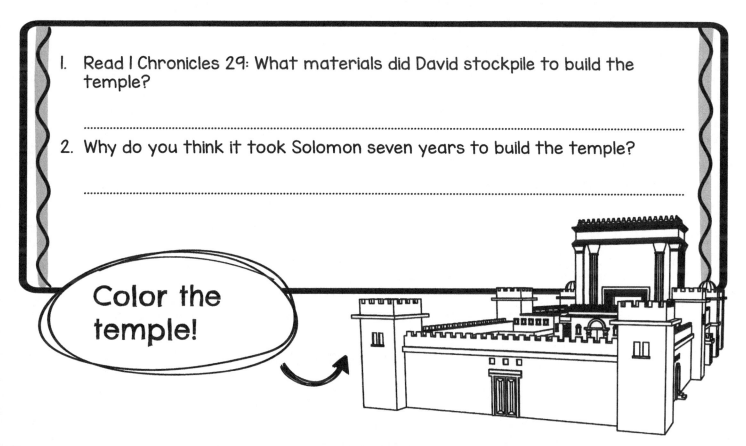

Color the temple!

When King Belshazzar saw the handwriting on the wall, he was very afraid! (Daniel 5:5-13) Unscramble the words to learn the people and objects mentioned in this Bible passage.

BELSHAZZAR!

azzhBaelsr ....

isfegnr ....

andaCshel ....

ginitwr ....

ladtspnam ....

nhad ....

llaw ....

aenDil ....

✳ Read about the king's party and the handwriting on the wall in Daniel 5.

Writing On the Wall

You will need:

1. Elmer's white glue or white school glue
2. Colored crayons
3. Two templates (see next pages)

Instructions:

1. Print or make copies of the page with the words MENE MENE TEKEL UPARSIN (one page for each child). Trace the letters with glue and allow to dry. Then give each child their own page.
2. Lay the page with the king on top.
3. Ask the children to color the wall with colored crayons. As they color the wall, the words will appear.

MENE

MENE

TEKEL

UPARSIN

Bible Pathway Adventures

Did you know?

The message on the wall was written in a language called Aramaic. It said: MENE, MENE, TEKEL, UPHARSIN, meaning: "God has numbered the days of your reign and brought it to an end. You have been weighed on the scales and found wanting. Your kingdom is divided and given to the Medes and Persians." (Daniel 5:24-26) The main difference between Aramaic and Hebrew was that Aramaic was the language of the Arameans (Syrians) while Hebrew was the language of the Hebrews (Israelites). Daniel was a Hebrew from the tribe of Judah.

Read the Aramaic alphabet on the following page.
Write the alphabet in the space below.

Aramaic alphabet

Although Old Persian was the Persians' native tongue, Aramaic was the administrative language of the empire. It was used to compose letters and messages. Aramaic is a Semitic language containing 22 characters. It has been written for over 3000 years and spoken for longer than that. It is one of the Northwest Semitic languages. The Semitic languages include Aramaic, Hebrew, Arabic and many others. Both Aramaic and Hebrew are closely related, with similar terminology. However, there are plenty of grammatical and lexical variations between these two languages.

aleph	beth	gimmel	daleth	he
waw	zayin	heth	teth	yodh
kaph	lamedh	mem	nun	samekh
ayin	pe	tsadi	qoph	res
sin	taw			

** Article adapted from Aramaic language Facts for Kids. Kiddle Encyclopedia.

The king's feast

The king was afraid because…

If this story was a book, the cover would look like…

Read Daniel 5:5-6. Draw the handwriting on the wall.

Read Daniel 5:25-28. Mene, Mene, Tekel, and Parsin means…

The Magi

The term *magi* was the name for priests and wise men among the Medes, Persians, Babylonians, and Chaldeans. They were an old and powerful priestly caste that had great knowledge of medicine, astronomy, and other sciences. They provided advice to the kings of the Babylonians, Medes, and Persians in divine and other daily matters. As a young man, Daniel was instructed in the ways and wisdom of the Chaldeans. In Daniel 1:17-20, 2:12-14, 24, and 27, Daniel and his three friends, Shadrach, Meshach, and Abednego were considered Magi.

There was no separation of church and state in Babylon. Daniel, who became the Chief Magi over the entire kingdom of Babylon (Daniel 5:11), was the boss of these magicians, astrologers, Chaldeans, and soothsayers. However, Daniel was faithful to God and did not practice astrology, divination, and magic like many other Magi. Daniel knew God had written His plan of Salvation in the heavens, so he practiced biblical astronomy (the Mazzaroth). Most other Magi practiced Babylonian astrology. These Magi were astrologers, heathen physicians, priests, and learned men. From them descended a line of pagan priests and sorcerers. They forecast events through the observation and interpretation of the stars, the sun, the moon, and the planets. In Deuteronomy 18:9-10, God forbids practicing this type of divination.

Color the magi!

The Magi

At the time of Daniel, Babylon was the intellectual center of western Asia, and the Chaldeans were renowned for their study and knowledge of astrology and astronomy. They kept detailed astronomical records for over 360 years, which today helps us understand how the Wise Men from the East recognized and followed the star that led them to Bethlehem.

1. Who were the Magi?

2. What was Daniel's job?

3. What is the difference between Biblical astronomy and Babylonian astronomy?

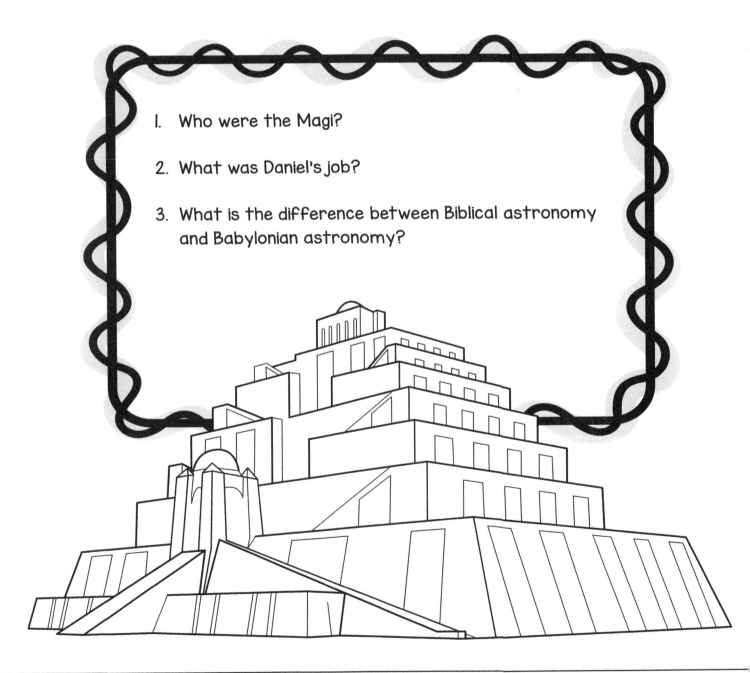

Daniel's gold chain

You will need:

1. Yellow or gold construction paper
2. Scissors (adults-only)
3. School glue or tape

Instructions:

1. Cut ten strips of construction paper. Each strip needs to be two inches wide and ten inches long.
2. Take one strip of construction paper, make it into a ring (chain), and tape together.
3. Slide your next strip of construction paper through the ring and tape or glue it into a 'chain'.
4. Repeat the process until you have a long chain of gold paper rings.

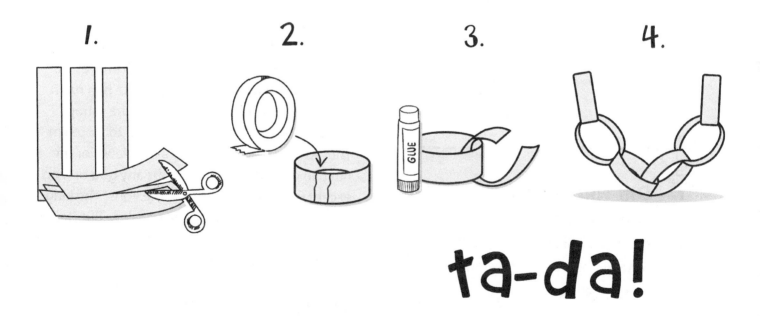

ta-da!

LESSON 3 | Lesson Plan
The satrap's plan

Teacher: _____

Today's Bible passage: Daniel 6:6-15

Welcome prayer:
Pray a simple prayer with the children before you begin the lesson.

Lesson objectives:
In this lesson, children will learn:
1. Why the satraps were jealous of Daniel
2. Why the king made a new law

Did You Know?
Kind Darius set up 20 different provinces called satrapies. Each satrapy was led by a governor called a satrap.

Bible lesson overview:
King Darius reigned over the kingdom of Babylon. He chose 120 satraps to help him rule, and three men to rule over the satraps. Daniel was one of these men. He was faithful and always did his best. The king was so impressed with Daniel that he planned to make him ruler over all the kingdom. But some of the satraps were jealous of Daniel, and wanted to stop him. They said to the king, "Make a new law: For the next 30 days, whoever petitions any god or man except you will be thrown to the lions." The king liked this idea! He signed the new law. But Daniel had courage. Every day, he continued to pray and thank God. When the satraps saw Daniel praying, they ran and told the king. The king liked Daniel but he could not change the law. Now he had to throw Daniel to the lions!

Let's Review:

Questions to ask your students:

1. Who was the king of Babylon?
2. What job did the king give Daniel?
3. Why were the satraps jealous of Daniel?
4. What new law did the king sign?
5. Why was the king upset when the satraps told him about Daniel?

 A memory verse to help children remember God's Word:

"Daniel got down on his knees three times a day and prayed and gave thanks before his God…" (Daniel 6:10)

 ## Activities:

Bible quiz: The satrap's plan

Bible word search puzzle: The satrap's plan

Comprehension worksheets: Babylon

Worksheet: A new law

Worksheet: Write your name in cuneiform

Worksheet: I am thankful…

Coloring page: Daniel prays and thanks God

Worksheet: Did You Know?

Worksheet: The Persian satrap

Worksheet: Design your own silver coin

Worksheet: True or false?

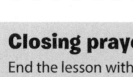

 ## Closing prayer:

End the lesson with a small prayer.

THE SATRAP'S PLAN

Read Daniel 1:3-6 and 6:1-15 (ESV).
Answer the questions below.

1. What job did King Darius give Daniel? ....

2. What job did the king plan to give Daniel? ....

3. What did the high officials and satraps try to do to Daniel? ....

4. What agreement did the high officials and satraps make? ....

5. Did the king sign the new law? ....

6. How did Daniel respond when he heard about the new law? ....

7. What did the officials do when they saw Daniel praying? ....

8. Was the king able to change the law of the Medes and Persians? ....

9. Daniel was of which tribe of Israel? ....

10. Why do you think the king was distressed when he heard about Daniel? ....

THE SATRAP'S PLAN

Read Daniel 6:1-5 (ESV).
Find and circle each of the words from the list below.

```
F P M C B V J N O R W N E V H D
O E E J C U E R F I N P C K C A
S T F E Z Y E H F C O Y P I K N
G I J R N K Z W I E X Y E N I I
A T Y U S D N A C T B O R J N E
G I D S B F D U I L E R S U G L
R O V A Z W I K A G A R I N D Q
E N M L K I Y R L O J W A C O P
E E T E X O R X A V P S N T M G
M K M M D T R A U E K A S I W M
E F S Q N E G M I R B T L O W E
N E C B M F S D E N U R I N M H
T L E J L T W D L O Q A O V A J
B A B Y L O N P K R V P N N A U
I B R P R A Y H V S U C S J B V
A R H E U K I N G D A R I U S G
```

KINGDOM   INJUNCTION   OFFICIAL   KING DARIUS
GOVERNORS   PRAY   AGREEMENT   SATRAP
PERSIANS   LIONS   JERUSALEM   DANIEL
MEDES   BABYLON   LAW   PETITION

Babylon

During its first thousand years, Babylon was a village. Later, it became a powerful city-state, the capital city, and the name of one of the greatest empires in history. It was known for its beautiful palaces, temples, and towers. For centuries, various tribes including the Kassites, the Chaldeans, the Aramaeans, and the Assyrians controlled the city. During that period, Babylon was regarded as a center of learning and culture.

After the last of the Assyrian rulers of Babylon died, Babylon became even wealthier and more important due to the influence of King Nebuchadnezzar II. He was celebrated as the builder who made Babylon the most splendid city in the world. Babylon lost its independence when Cyrus the Great of Persia invaded the land. But it continued to be a center of trade and culture. However, like all ancient empires, Babylon eventually declined. Its buildings crumbled and were used to provide bricks for other structures. The city was eventually reduced to ruins.

1. Read Daniel 1. Why was Daniel taken to Babylon?

2. Find five Bible verses that mention Babylon.

3. Why do you think all empires eventually decline?

A Babylonian

King Nebuchadnezzar

Nebuchadnezzar's father died while he was away at battle. He quickly returned to Babylon and claimed his crown.

To defend Babylon, King Nebuchadnezzar II built a moat around the city.

After King Nebuchadnezzar II died, the empire began to fall apart. In 529 BC, the Persians conquered Babylon and made it part of the Persian Empire.

Some historians believe King Nebuchadnezzar II built the Hanging Gardens of Babylon. According to historical records, the gardens included a large series of terraces up to 75 feet high. They were covered in trees, flowers, and plants.

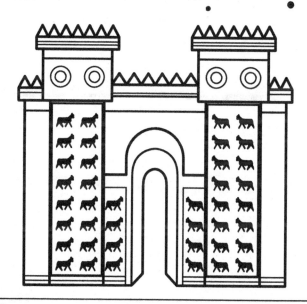

A new law

Read Daniel 6:1-15. Write the king's new law on the cuneiform tablet below.

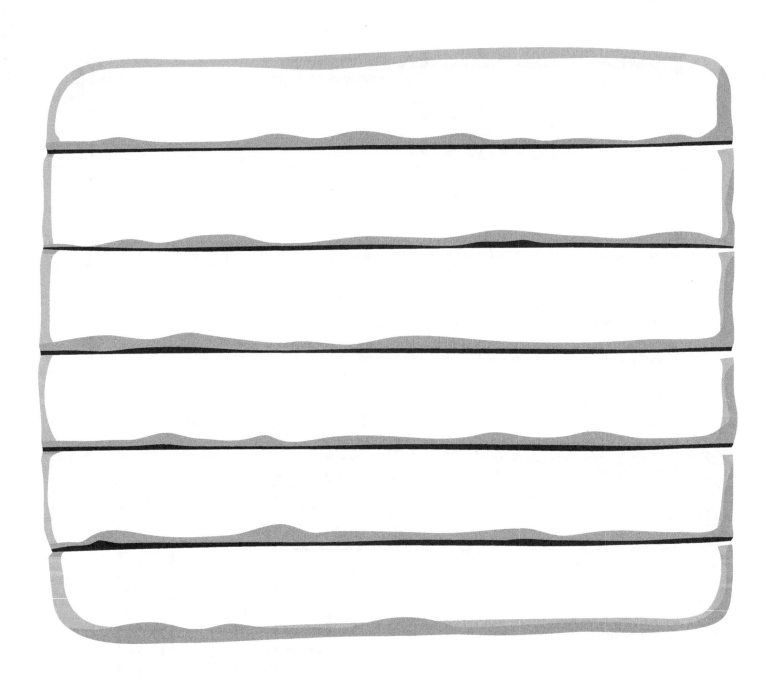

Write your name in Cuneiform

Cuneiform was developed by the Sumerians. It was the first system of writing, and included hundreds of pictographs. Because there were so many symbols, it was the job of a scribe to learn to read and write, and record laws, treaties, and religious customs. When Daniel lived in Babylon, this is the writing system used to create official documents.

Write your name in cuneiform:

I am thankful...

"When Daniel knew the document had been signed, he went to his house where he had windows in his upper chamber open toward Jerusalem. He got down on his knees three times a day and prayed and gave thanks before his God…"
(Daniel 6:10)

Why do you think Daniel continued to pray and thank God after King Darius signed the new law?

....

What do you think Daniel prayed <u>three</u> times a day?

....

....

JUDAH

Read Daniel 1:6.

Daniel was of the tribe of

"He got down on his knees three times a day and prayed and gave thanks before his God..."

(Daniel 6:10)

Did you know?

King Darius ruled the Persian Empire for 35 years. He was the third king in the Achaemenian family. He controlled the empire by establishing a new type of government; he set up many different provinces called satrapies. Each satrapy was led by a governor called a satrap. It was Daniel's job to oversee these men. The satrap had extensive authority. They collected taxes, minted coins, and kept law and order in his region. To keep an eye on each satrap, the king appointed a military commander for each satrapy.

Research the type of clothing were worn by the ancient Persians.
Use this space to draw a Persian satrap.

The Persian satrap

Satraps were local rulers appointed by the king to govern individual provinces. Their job was to mint coins, collect taxes and tributes, control local officials, and enforce law and order in the province. The satrap even had a local army, although the garrisons in the citadels and the regular army were under the command of the king. Sometimes the satraps rebelled. Under kings like Cyrus the Great or Darius the Great, the satrapy system worked well. Under other kings, the satraps rebelled repeatedly. At times, the office of satrap was passed down through the family, and some satrap dynasties continued for many generations.

Because satraps could not always be trusted, officials were appointed to oversee them, and make sure they did not steal taxes and tributes, or plot against the king. In Daniel 6:1-15, the satraps introduced an ordinance that allowed them to condemn Daniel to death. Did they do this because Daniel was the 'eyes of the king' who would report any dishonest or illegal activity by a satrap? What do you think?

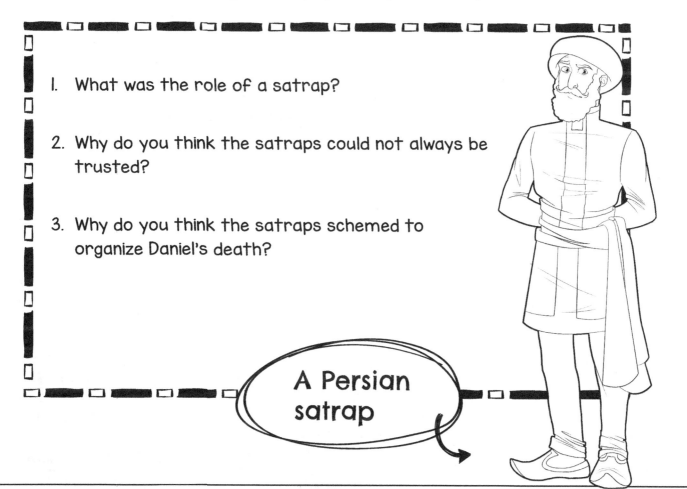

1. What was the role of a satrap?

2. Why do you think the satraps could not always be trusted?

3. Why do you think the satraps schemed to organize Daniel's death?

A Persian satrap

DESIGN YOUR OWN SILVER COIN

A Persian satrap had the right to mint coins in his name, except for gold coins which were exclusively minted by the king or emperor. Satraps often depicted themselves on coins. They combined Persian and Greek imagery, showing a satrap's head on one side, and a local image on the reverse side. Imagine you are a Persian satrap. Design your own silver coin.

Design both sides of your coin in the spaces below.
Use your imagination!

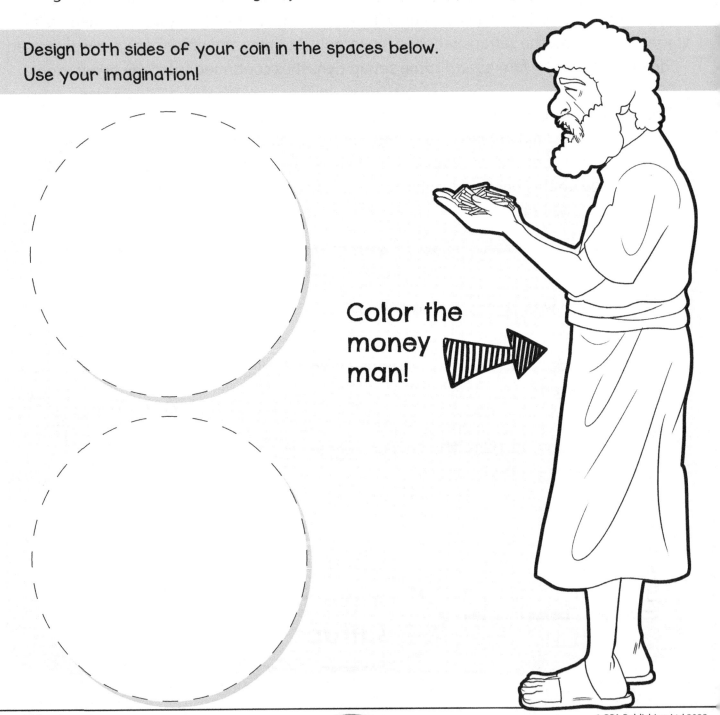

Color the money man!

TRUE OR FALSE?

Are the statements below TRUE or FALSE?
Read Daniel 6:1-15 (ESV). Circle the correct box below.

Darius set over the kingdom 140 satraps	**TRUE** | **FALSE**
The officials and satraps wanted to get Daniel into trouble	**TRUE** | **FALSE**
The officials and satraps told the king to make a new law	**TRUE** | **FALSE**
After the new law had been signed, Daniel stopped praying to God	**TRUE** | **FALSE**
The king abolished the new law	**TRUE** | **FALSE**
The king was happy to have Daniel thrown to the lions	**TRUE** | **FALSE**

Are these statements true or false?

LESSON 4 | Lesson Plan
Thrown to the lions

Teacher: _____

Today's Bible passage: Daniel 6:15-23

Welcome prayer:
Pray a simple prayer with the children before you begin the lesson.

Lesson objectives:
In this lesson, children will learn:
1. Why King Darius had Daniel thrown to the lions
2. How God protected Daniel from the lions

Did You Know?
In Babylon, anything marked with the royal seal was like a direct command from the king. His subjects had to act accordingly.

Bible lesson overview:
The king did not want to throw Daniel into the lion's den. But he could not change the law of the Medes and Persians. "Throw Daniel to the lions," he said to his men. The men obeyed the king. They threw Daniel into a den full of lions. The king sealed the door shut with his own signet ring. But Daniel was not afraid. He trusted God to protect him. That night, God sent an angel to shut the lion's mouths. The lions did not hurt Daniel because he trusted God. Early the next morning, the king went to see Daniel. "My God sent His angel and shut the lions' mouths. They did not hurt me," Daniel told him. The king was pleased. "Take Daniel out of the den," he commanded.

Let's Review:

Questions to ask your students:

1. Why was the king unable to change the law?
2. How did the king seal the door?
3. How did God protect Daniel from the lions?
4. Why did the lions not hurt Daniel?
5. Why was the king pleased to see that Daniel was alive?

 A memory verse to help children remember God's Word:

"My God sent His angel and shut the lions' mouths, and they have not harmed me, because I was found blameless before Him…" (Daniel 6:22)

 Activities:

Bible quiz: Thrown to the lions
What's the word? Daniel and the lions
Worksheet: What is fasting?
Worksheet: The royal seal
Worksheet: Into the den
Coloring worksheet: Daniel and the lions
Worksheet: All about lions
Coloring page: Thrown to the lions
Worksheet: Who do I trust?
Labyrinth: Where's Daniel?
Newspaper worksheet: Daniel thrown to the lions
Worksheet: Perfect peace…

 Closing prayer:

End the lesson with a small prayer.

THROWN TO THE LIONS

Read Daniel 6:1-23 (ESV).
Answer the questions below.

1. Who plotted to kill Daniel? ....

2. What happened to Daniel after he gave thanks to God by his

    open window? ....

3. Why was Daniel thrown to the lions? ....

4. Which king had Daniel thrown to the lions? ....

5. How was the lion's den sealed? ....

6. What did the king do that night? ....

7. How was Daniel protected from the lions in the den? ....

8. Why did God protect Daniel? ....

9. Why was the king happy to see Daniel the next morning? ....

10. What was done to the men who had accused Daniel? ....

DANIEL AND THE LIONS

Read Daniel 6:16-23 (ESV). Fill in the blanks below.

66 The king commanded, and .... was brought and cast into the den of .... The king declared to Daniel, "May your God, whom you serve continually, deliver you!" A stone was brought and laid on the mouth of the den, and the king .... it with his own signet and with the .... of his lords, that nothing might be changed concerning Daniel. Then the king went to his .... and spent the night ....; no diversions were brought to him, and sleep fled from him. At break of day, the king arose and went in haste to the den of lions. As he came near to the den where Daniel was, he cried out in a tone of anguish. The king declared to Daniel, "O Daniel, ... of the living God, has your God, whom you serve continually, been able to deliver you from the lions?" Daniel said to the ...., "O king, live forever! My God sent his .... and shut the lions' mouths, and they have not harmed me, because I was found .... before him; and also before you, O king, I have done no harm." The king was exceedingly glad and .... Daniel be taken up out of the den. Daniel was taken up out of the den, and no kind of harm was found on him, because he had .... in his God. **99**

DANIEL	BLAMELESS
SEALED	KING
PALACE	COMMANDED
FASTING	TRUSTED
SERVANT	SIGNET
ANGEL	LIONS

What is fasting?

*"King Darius went to his palace and spent the night fasting;
no diversions were brought to him, and sleep fled from him."*

(Daniel 6:18)

Fasting is when someone does not eat or drink for a specified period.
Some people may fast for a certain number of hours per day, while others may fast
for longer. There are many different kinds of fasting. Do you fast? Why / why not?

1. Why do you think King Darius fasted all night?

    ....

2. Name three famous Bible characters who fasted.

    ....

Color
the king!

The royal seal

Persian kings used clay tablets, the cuneiform script, and seals to help them administer their kingdom or empire. Royal seals were often made out of gold. Whoever had a copy of this seal, usually in the shape of a golden signet ring, was acting on behalf of the king. Any clay tablet displaying an impression of the royal seal was like a direct command of the king. His commands could not be refused, and the king's subjects were forced to act accordingly.

In Egypt, the Agate Cylinder Seal was discovered in a tomb at Thebes, the cemetery of Memphis. It was the official seal of Darius I, and was engraved with a picture of the king hunting lions from his chariot. The cuneiform inscription along one side was written in three languages: Old Persian, Elamite and Babylonian (the three official languages of the empire), and translates as 'Darius the great king'. During Darius' reign, Egypt was part of the Persian Empire, and Memphis was a seat of the Persian administration.

Imagine you are the king of Persia. Design your own royal seal.
Include your name in cuneiform, your portrait, and an animal.

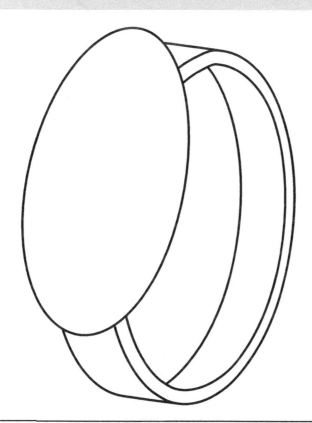

Into the den...

Daniel was thrown into a den of lions. Do you think he took anything with him?
Think about life in Babylon and make a list of items you would take into
a lion's den. Draw some of the items inside the bag. Use your imagination!

1. ....

2. ....

3. ....

4. ....

5. ....

6. ....

7. ....

8. ....

9. ....

10...

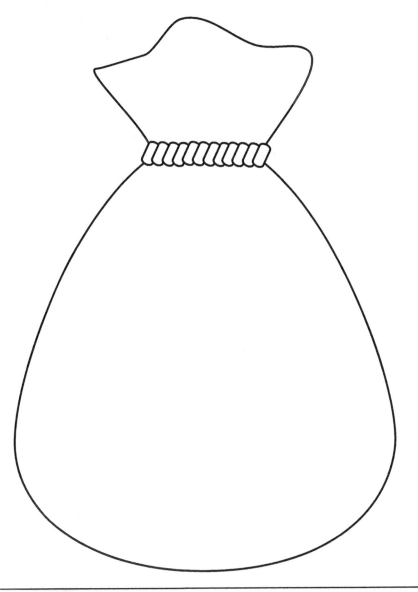

Daniel and the lions

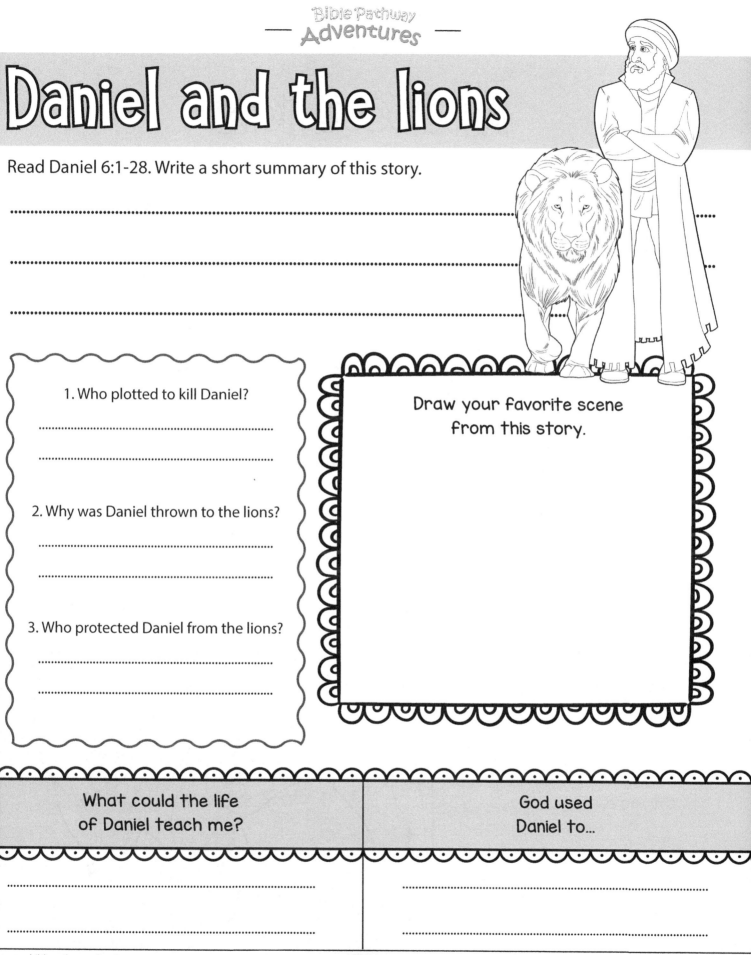

Read Daniel 6:1-28. Write a short summary of this story.

....

....

....

1. Who plotted to kill Daniel?

....

....

2. Why was Daniel thrown to the lions?

....

....

3. Who protected Daniel from the lions?

....

....

Draw your favorite scene
from this story.

What could the life
of Daniel teach me?

God used
Daniel to...

....

....

All about lions

Lions live in groups that are called prides. An average pride includes 15 lions; five to 10 females with their young, and two or three males that are usually brothers or pride mates. Each pride has a home area that is called its territory. A territory can be as large as 100 square miles, and lions will not allow strange animals to hunt in their territory. The females do the hunting, but the males will help if the females have difficulty killing an animal. The male is the first to eat. When the male is finished, the females and the cubs may eat. While the lionesses hunt and care for the young, the males patrol the territory and protect the pride. However, lions love to rest and relax. They spend time rubbing heads, purring and licking each other, and sometimes squabbling and fighting. They can spend 16 to 20 hours a day sleeping and resting.

Lions appear in heraldry more often than any other animal. They symbolise courage, valour and royalty. One reason why lions are shown in many different ways is because when heraldry developed, a lot of people wanted a lion on their coat of arms, but no two coats of arms could the same.

Why do you think male lions are the first to eat?

....

....

Write five statements about lions:

....

....

....

....

....

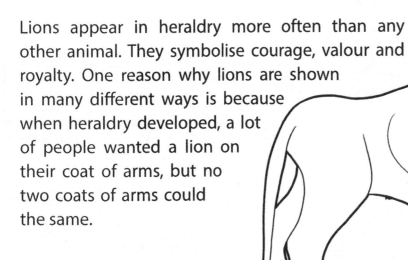

"The king commanded, and Daniel was brought and cast into the den of lions."

(Daniel 6:16)

Who do I trust?

Trust is believing someone will do what they say. Daniel trusted God to save him from the lions (Daniel 6:23). Write a paragraph about someone you trust. Why do you trust them?

....

....

....

....

....

....

....

....

....

....

....

....

WHERE'S DANIEL?

Daniel was thrown in the lion's den. The king was worried! (Daniel 6:19).
Help the king get to Daniel.

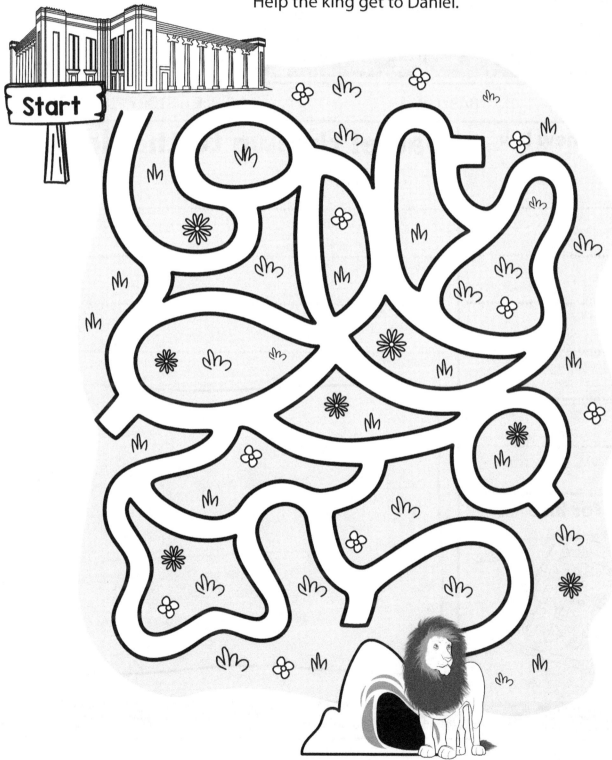

City of Babylon

The Babylonian Times

DANIEL 6   BABYLONIA   A BIBLE HISTORY PUBLICATION

King signs new law

....

....

....

....

....

....

Scribes for hire

Daniel thrown to the lions

....

....

....

....

 # PERFECT PEACE...

Even though Daniel was in a tough situation, he trusted God. Do you think Daniel had peace inside the lion's den? Read Isaiah 26:3 and write a paragraph to describe a time you trusted God and received His peace. Color the illustration at the bottom of the page.

LESSON 5 | **Lesson Plan**
The king's letter

Teacher: _____

Today's Bible passage: Daniel 6:23-28

Welcome prayer:
Pray a simple prayer with the children before you begin the lesson.

Lesson objectives:
In this lesson, children will learn:
1. How the king punished the satraps
2. Why the king wrote to all the people that dwell on the earth

Did You Know?
Archaeologists have found the ruins of Babylon in modern-day Iraq.

Bible lesson overview:
Daniel told King Darius that God had saved him from the lions. The king was happy that Daniel was alive! He commanded that Daniel be taken up out of the den. But the king was not pleased with the satraps and officials who tried to have Daniel killed. These satraps, officials, and their families were thrown into the lions' den. The king wrote a letter to everyone telling them that Yahweh, the God of Abraham, Isaac, and Jacob was the one true God. He wrote, "I am making a new law. Daniel's God is the living God. He saved Daniel from the lions."

Let's Review:

Questions to ask your students:

1. What did Daniel tell the king?
2. What happened to the satraps, officials and their families?
3. To whom did the king write a letter?
4. What was the king's decree in his letter?
5. What has this story taught you about trust?

A memory verse to help children remember God's Word:

"God delivers and rescues; He works signs and wonders in heaven and on earth, He who has saved Daniel from the power of the lions." (Daniel 6:27)

Activities:

What's the word? Into the den!

Bible crossword puzzle: The king's letter

Worksheet: Write a letter!

Coloring page: The king's messengers

Worksheet: The royal postal service

Worksheet: The king's letter

Let's learn Hebrew: Daniel

Comprehension worksheets: Babylon discovered?

Read and sequence worksheet: Daniel and the lions

My Bible notes

Closing prayer:

End the lesson with a small prayer.

INTO THE DEN!

Read Daniel 6:24-28 (ESV). Fill in the blanks below.

" The king commanded, and those men who had maliciously .... Daniel were brought and cast into the .... of lions—they, their children, and their wives. Before they reached the bottom of the den, the lions .... them and broke all their bones in pieces. Then King .... wrote to all the peoples, nations, and .... that dwell in all the earth: "Peace be multiplied to you. I make a decree, that in all my royal dominion people are to tremble and fear before the God of Daniel, for he is the .... God, enduring forever; his .... shall never be destroyed, and his .... shall be to the end. He .... and rescues; he works signs and .... in heaven and on earth, he who has saved Daniel from the power of the lions. So this .... prospered during the .... of Darius and the reign of Cyrus the Persian. **"**

WONDERS   DOMINION
ACCUSED   DEN
DARIUS   LANGUAGES
LIVING   KINGDOM
DANIEL   DELIVERS
REIGN   OVERPOWERED

THE KING'S LETTER

Read Daniel 6:16-28 (ESV). Complete the crossword below.

ACROSS

4) The God of Daniel is the _____ God.
5) No harm was found on Daniel because he _____ God.
6) Daniel _____ during the reign of Darius and Cyrus the Persian.
8) The lions broke all their _____ into pieces.

DOWN

1) Daniel was thrown into the lions' _____.
2) He delivers and rescues; he works signs and _____ in heaven and on earth.
3) His kingdom shall never be _____.
4) The men who accused Daniel were cast into the den of _____.
6) "_____ be multiplied to you."
7) Which king wrote to all the peoples, nations, and languages?

Write a letter!

Imagine you are King Darius. Write a letter to everyone in your kingdom, telling them how God saved Daniel from the lions. Include all the words below in your letter.

_____

_____

_____

_____

_____

_____

_____

_____

_____

| LIONS | ANGEL | KINGDOM | DELIVERS |
| DANIEL | DEN | SAVED | POWER |

"King Darius wrote to all the peoples, nations, and languages that dwell in all the earth..."

(Daniel 6:25)

The royal postal service

At its peak, under the reign of Darius the Great, the Persian Empire stretched from Greece to India. To keep close contact with all the provinces, Darius connected cities with a network of stone-paved roads, and created a postal system that spanned the empire. This postal system was powered by horses that worked on a relay system, making journeys along these roads quick and efficient. Messengers (known as *pirradaziš* in Old Persian) could deliver messages from one end of the empire to the other in a matter of days.

Each road had a network of postal stations where messengers would change horses as letters made their way to the king. Every twenty-four kilometers was a military post and a caravanserai *(an inn)*. Each messenger would ride to the next station, where a fresh horse was waiting. When he reached the end of his shift, a fresh messenger was waiting, keeping the mail moving constantly towards its destination. Some historians believe it was possible to send a message from Susa to Sardis (western Turkey) in seven and nine days, following the Royal Road. While this road was efficient and effective at delivering messages, it was only used for administrative purposes. Private citizens could not use the postal system.

THE ROYAL ROAD

Describe a day in the life of a pirradaziš.

....

....

....

....

....

....

The king's letter

Daniel 6:26-27

Fear and respect the God of Daniel,
for he is the living God,
enduring forever;
his kingdom shall never be destroyed,
and his dominion shall be to the end.
He delivers and rescues;
he works signs and wonders
in heaven and on earth,
he who saved Daniel
from the power of the lions.

✰ DANIYEL ✰

The Hebrew name for Daniel is Daniyel. Daniel was an Israelite from the tribe of Judah (Daniel 1:6). He was deported to Babylon after King Nebuchadnezzar destroyed Jerusalem. There he worked for the king and shared God's wisdom with him. After he interpreted the king's strange dream, he was given many gifts and made a ruler over the whole province of Babylon. Later, King Darius had Daniel thrown into the lions' den. But God shut the lions' mouths and they did not hurt him, because he had trusted in his God.

Daniyel

דָּנִיֵּאל

Daniel

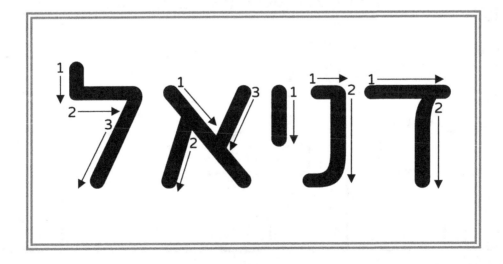

LET'S WRITE!

Practice writing Daniel's Hebrew name on the lines below.

דָּנִיֵּאל

דָּנִיֵּאל

Try this on your own.
Remember that Hebrew is read from RIGHT to LEFT.

Babylon discovered?

Babylon was an empire in ancient Mesopotamia, a region now part of modern-day Iraq. According to historians, the city of Babylon was originally named Bab-Ilu, meaning "gate of the gods." The Hebrews called it Babel, but in the Greek and Latin languages it was known as Babylon. The original city stood on the west bank of the Euphrates River, and was shaped like a square surrounded by a massive towered wall. Huge palaces and temples were constructed, and there was even a terraced tower (ziggurat) built in seven receding stories with a sloping ramp spiraling around it to the top. Some scholars believe this may have been the original Tower of Babel, but it could have been one of many artificial "holy mountains" in and around Babylon.

A German archaeologist rediscovered Babylon's remains at the end of the 19th century near Mosul in Iraq. Excavations lasted until 1917, and the famous Ishtar Gate was moved to the Pergamon Museum in Berlin. The Iraqi governments' restoration program began in 1957, but during the American invasion of Iraq the site was used as an army base, further damaging its ruins. Today you can visit the ruins of Babylon near the town of al Hillah.

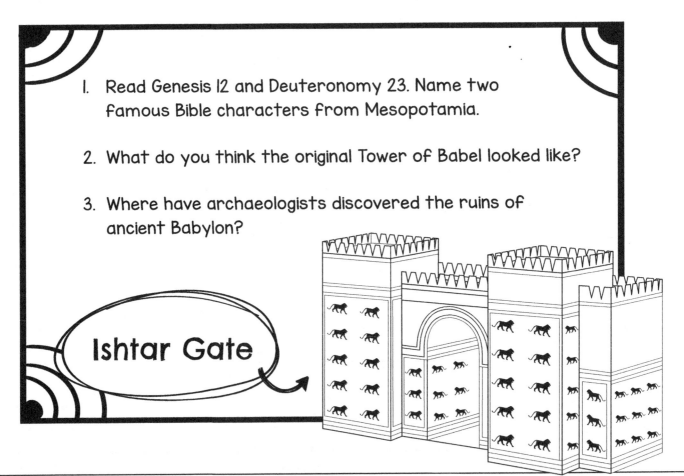

1. Read Genesis 12 and Deuteronomy 23. Name two famous Bible characters from Mesopotamia.

2. What do you think the original Tower of Babel looked like?

3. Where have archaeologists discovered the ruins of ancient Babylon?

Ishtar Gate

Amazing facts about Babylon

Ancient Babylon is covered by modern-day Iraq, Iran, Syria, and Turkey. The ancient city of Babylon was discovered 59 miles southwest of modern-day Baghdad.

The Babylonians wore clothes made from woven fabric, and shoes and sandals made from leather.

The ancient Babylonians invented the sundial to tell time.

Babylonians ate stews filled with savory meats, herbaceous herbs, and earthy vegetables. They also enjoyed melons, plums, prunes, and dates.

Scholars believe the Hanging Gardens of Babylon were built in Babylon. While there is no proof they existed, they are considered one of the seven wonders of the ancient world.

DANIEL AND THE LIONS

Read Daniel 1:1-6:28 (ESV). Place the events in the correct order.

A. .... The high officials and satraps could find no fault with Daniel.

B. .... Daniel continued to pray and thank God three times a day.

C. .... Daniel helped King Nebuchadnezzar understand his dream about a statue.

D. .... King Darius wrote to everyone in the kingdom, telling them about the God of Daniel.

E. .... King Darius had Daniel thrown into a den of lions.

F. .... Daniel interpreted the handwriting on the wall of the palace.

G. .... King Darius made Daniel the third ruler in the kingdom.

H. .... Daniel was taken prisoner to Babylon.

I. .... King Darius signed a new law. People could only petition him for 30 days.

J. .... God sent an angel to shut the lions' mouths in the den. Daniel was not harmed.

⭐ My Bible notes ⭐

Draw your favorite scene from the story of Daniel and the lions.

The life of Daniel teaches me…

_____

_____

_____

_____

_____

ANSWER KEY

Lesson One: The king's dream
Let's Review:
1. Daniel and his friends were taken captive by the Babylonian army, and taken back to Babylon
2. King Nebuchadnezzar
3. In his dream, the king saw a gigantic statue made of four metals (a head of gold, arms and chest of silver, belly and thighs of bronze, legs of iron, and feet of mingled iron and clay.) A great stone, not cut by human hands, fell on the feet of the statue and destroyed it, and the rock became a mountain that filled the whole world
4. Daniel helped the king understand his dream
5. The king made Daniel ruler over the province of Babylon, and chief governor over all the magi

Worksheet: The southern kingdom
1. Tribe of Judah: David, Solomon, Daniel, Hananiah, Mishael and Azariah, Amos, Isaiah, Joel, Micah, Obadiah, Zechariah, Zephaniah, and Yeshua
2. Tribe of Benjamin: Mordecai, Esther, and the apostle Paul (Sha'ul)

Bible quiz: Daniel in Babylon
1. People of Israel from the royal family and of the nobility. Youths without blemish, endowed with knowledge, understanding, and intelligence
2. Daniel, Shadrach, Meshach, and Abednego
3. Daniel resolved not to defile himself with the king's food or wine
4. God gave Daniel learning and skill in all literature and wisdom, and understanding in all visions and dreams
5. The magicians, the enchanters, the sorcerers, and the Chaldeans could not interpret the king's dream
6. Because the wise men could not interpret the king's dream
7. In a vision during the night
8. Belteshazzar
9. Iron, clay, bronze, silver, gold
10. The king gave Daniel many gifts, and made him ruler over the province of Babylon, and chief prefect over the magi

What's the word? Daniel's faithfulness
Daniel asked the chief of the eunuchs to allow him not to defile himself. God gave Daniel favor and compassion in the sight of the chief. The chief said to Daniel, "I fear the king, who assigned your food and drink; for why should he see that you were in worse condition than the youths who are of your own age? You would endanger my head with the king." Daniel said to the steward whom the chief of the eunuchs had assigned over Daniel, Hananiah, Mishael, and Azariah, "Test your servants for ten days; give us vegetables to eat and water to drink. Let our appearance and the appearance of the youths who eat the king's food be observed by you, and deal with your servants according to what you see." He listened to them and tested them for ten days. At the end of ten days it was seen that they were better in appearance and fatter in flesh than the youths who ate the king's food. The steward took away their food and the wine they were to drink, and gave them vegetables. As for these four youths, God gave them learning and skill in all literature and wisdom, and Daniel had understanding in all visions and dreams. At the end of the time, when the king had commanded they should be brought in, the chief of the eunuchs brought them before Nebuchadnezzar. The king spoke with them, and among all of them none was found like Daniel, Hananiah, Mishael, and Azariah. In every matter of wisdom and understanding… he found them ten times better than all the magicians and enchanters in his kingdom.

Bible word search puzzle: The king's dream

```
T L N H K F E U D R E A M O J A
M P D W J N Q J Q V R W E H R T
H R K U I J A A X I Z L V K P C
E B B V Y S J R F S J X I N B P
C L A Y K U E A K I N Z E O R B
I R O N S X L M E O L K P W O A
A C I D P K D A E N C N T L N J
R O S K A D Q I C N X I D E Z P
I L Y D N N X C M C R G K D E G
O E T K Z C I B Y W R A A G A C
C B F B P J E E V X A O J E H G
H U G M Y P K Z L U N B W J O O
I N T E R P R E T A T I O N C L
C H A L D E A N S X S T O N E D
U N E B U C H A D N E Z Z A R T
R E S A W I N S T A T U E R B A
```

Worksheet: The king's dream
1. A giant statue
2. The wise men could not interpret the king's dream
3. God gave Daniel a vision during the night

Comprehension worksheets: The king's dream

1. King Nebuchadnezzar ruled the Babylonian Empire for 43 years
2. The construction of a double wall ten miles long that surrounded the city of Babylon, and a magnificent entry called the Ishtar Gate. Many scholars believe it was Nebuchadnezzar who built the Hanging Gardens of Babylon
3. Nebuchadnezzar II was most famous for conquering Judah and the destruction of Jerusalem
4. King Cyrus of Persia allowed the Hebrews to return to the land of Israel

Lesson Two: Handwriting on the wall
Let's Review:

1. Important officials of Babylon
2. The king drank from cups stolen from the temple in Jerusalem
3. No, God was not pleased with the king's behavior because he used the gold and silver vessels from the temple in Jerusalem at his feast
4. "Mene, God has numbered the days of your kingdom and brought it to an end; Tekel, you have been weighed in the balances and found wanting; Peres, your kingdom is divided and given to the Medes and Persians."
5. Daniel was clothed with purple, a chain of gold was put around his neck, and a proclamation was made about him, that he should be the third ruler in the kingdom

Bible quiz: Handwriting on the wall

1. King Belshazzar
2. The temple in Jerusalem
3. The fingers of a human hand
4. The king's limbs gave way and his knees knocked together
5. Mene, mene, tekel, parsin
6. The magicians, the Chaldeans and the astrologers (the wise men)
7. Daniel
8. God has numbered the days of your kingdom and brought it to an end; you have been weighed in the balances and found wanting; your kingdom is divided and given to the Medes and Persians.
9. Daniel was clothed with purple, a chain of gold was put around his neck, and a proclamation was made about him, that he should be the third ruler in the kingdom of Babylon
10. King Darius

Worksheet: Temple in Jerusalem

1. King David stored gold, silver, iron, timber and stone to build a temple
2. Ask children to answer this question

Bible word unscramble: Handwriting on the wall

Belshazzar
fingers
Chaldeans
writing
lampstand
hand
wall
Daniel

Worksheet: The Magi

1. The Magi were the priests and wise men among the Medes, Persians, Babylonians, and Chaldeans. They were an old and powerful priestly caste that had great knowledge of medicine, astronomy, and other sciences
2. Daniel became the Chief Magi over the entire kingdom of Babylon (Daniel 5:11), and was the boss of these magicians, astrologers, Chaldeans, and soothsayers
3. Biblical astronomy is the understanding that God's plan of salvation is written in the heavens (the Mazzaroth). Babylonian astronomy is a type of divination that involves the forecasting of earthly and human events through the observation and interpretation of the stars, the sun, the moon, and the planets. God forbids practicing divination in Deuteronomy 18:9-10

Lesson Three: The satrap's plan
Let's Review:

1. King Darius was the king of Babylon
2. The king made Daniel ruler over the satraps
3. The king planned to make Daniel ruler over the kingdom
4. For the next 30 days, whoever prays to any god or man except the king will be thrown into the lions' den
5. The king was upset because he could not change the law of the Medes and Persians. He was forced to have Daniel thrown to the lions

Bible quiz: The satrap's plan

1. Daniel was a high official
2. The king planned to make Daniel ruler over the whole kingdom
3. The high officials and satraps tried to find a ground for complaint against Daniel
4. The king should establish a new law, that whoever prays to any god or man for 30 days (except the king) should be thrown into the lions' den
5. Yes
6. He went home and continued praying to God
7. The officials told the king that Daniel had broken the law
8. No, the king could not change the law of the Medes and Persians
9. Daniel was of the tribe of Judah (Daniel 1:3-6)
10. Daniel was a faithful servant to the king

Bible word search puzzle: The satrap's plan

```
T  L  N  H  K  F  E  U  D  R  E  A  M  O  J  A
M  P  D  W  J  N  Q  J  Q  V  R  W  E  H  R  T
H  R  K  U  J  A  A  X  I  Z  L  V  K  P  C
E  B  B  V  Y  S  J  R  F  S  J  X  I  N  B  P
C  L  A  Y  K  U  E  A  K  I  N  Z  E  O  R  B
I  R  O  N  S  X  L  M  E  O  L  K  P  W  O  A
A  C  I  D  P  K  D  A  E  N  C  N  T  L  N  J
R  O  S  K  A  D  Q  I  C  N  X  I  D  E  Z  P
I  L  Y  D  N  N  X  C  M  C  R  G  K  D  E  G
O  E  T  K  Z  C  I  B  Y  W  R  A  A  G  A  C
C  B  F  B  P  J  E  E  V  X  A  O  J  E  H  G
H  U  G  M  Y  P  K  Z  L  U  N  B  W  J  O  O
I  N  T  E  R  P  R  E  T  A  T  I  O  N  C  L
C  H  A  L  D  E  A  N  S  X  S  T  O  N  E  D
U  N  E  B  U  C  H  A  D  N  E  Z  Z  A  R  T
R  E  S  A  W  I  N  S  T  A  T  U  E  R  B  A
```

Worksheet: True or false?

Darius set over the kingdom 140 satraps: False
The officials and satraps wanted to get Daniel into trouble: True
The officials and satraps told the king to make a new law: True
After the new law had been signed, Daniel stopped praying to God: False
The king abolished the new law: False
The king was happy to have Daniel thrown to the lions: False

Lesson Four: Thrown to the lions
Let's Review:

1. It was a law of the Medes and Persians that no injunction or ordinance that the king established could be changed
2. The king sealed the door with his signet ring
3. God sent an angel to shut the lions' mouths
4. The lions didn't hurt Daniel because he trusted God
5. The king liked Daniel and did not want the lions to kill him

Bible quiz: Thrown to the lions

1. A group of satraps
2. Daniel was thrown into the lions' den
3. Daniel was thrown to the lions for praying to Yahweh, the god of Abraham, Isaac and Jacob
4. King Darius
5. With a large stone and the king's signet
6. That night, the king fasted and did not sleep
7. An angel of God shut the lion's mouths
8. God protected Daniel because Daniel trusted God
9. King Darius liked Daniel
10. Daniel's accusers were thrown into the lions' den

What's the word? Daniel and the lions

The king commanded, and Daniel was brought and cast into the den of lions. The king declared to Daniel, "May your God, whom you serve continually, deliver you!" A stone was brought and laid on the mouth of the den, and the king sealed it with his own signet and with the signet of his lords, that nothing might be changed concerning Daniel. Then the king went to his palace and spent the night fasting; no diversions were brought to him, and sleep fled from him. At break of day, the king arose and went in haste to the den of lions. As he came near to the den where Daniel was, he cried out in a tone of anguish. The king declared to Daniel, "O Daniel, servant of the living God, has your God, whom you serve continually, been able to deliver you from the lions?" Daniel said to the king, "O king, live forever! My God sent his angel and shut the lions' mouths, and they have not harmed me, because I was found blameless before him; and also before you, O king, I have done no harm." The king was exceedingly glad and commanded Daniel be taken up out of the den. Daniel was taken up out of the den, and no kind of harm was found on him, because he had trusted in his God.

Worksheet: What is fasting?

Answer #2: Bible characters who fasted include the Ninevites, Ahab, David, Daniel, Nehemiah, Anna the prophetess, Moses, Yeshua (Jesus), and the early church in the Book of Acts

Worksheet: All about lions

1. Lions live in groups that are called prides.
2. An average pride includes 15 lions; five to 10 females with their young, and two or three males that are usually brothers or pride mates
3. Each pride has a home area that is called its territory. A territory can be as large as 100 square miles
4. Lions will not allow strange animals to hunt in their territory
5. The females do the hunting, but the males will help if the females have difficulty killing an animal
6. A male lion is the first to eat. When the male is finished, the females and the cubs may eat. While the lionesses hunt and care for the young, the males patrol the territory and protect the pride
7. Lions love to rest and relax. They spend time rubbing heads, purring and licking each other, and sometimes squabbling and fighting
8. Lions can sleep and rest 16 to 20 hours a day
9. Lions appear in heraldry more often than any other animal
10. Lions symbolise courage, valour and royalty
11. One reason why lions are shown in many different ways is because when heraldry developed, a lot of people wanted a lion on their coat of arms, but no two coats of arms could be the same

Lesson Five: The king's letter
Let's Review:
1. Daniel told the king that God sent His angel to shut the lions' mouths
2. The king had the satraps, officials and their families thrown to the lions
3. The king wrote a letter to all the peoples of the earth
4. The God of Daniel is the living God. His kingdom shall never be destroyed
5. Ask children to answer this question

What's the word? Into the den!
The king commanded, and those men who had maliciously accused Daniel were brought and cast into the den of lions—they, their children, and their wives. Before they reached the bottom of the den, the lions overpowered them and broke all their bones in pieces. Then King Darius wrote to all the peoples, nations, and languages that dwell in all the earth: "Peace be multiplied to you. I make a decree, that in all my royal dominion people are to tremble and fear before the God of Daniel, for he is the living God, enduring forever; his kingdom shall never be destroyed, and his dominion shall be to the end. He delivers and rescues; he works signs and wonders in heaven and on earth, he who has saved Daniel from the power of the lions. So this Daniel prospered during the reign of Darius and the reign of Cyrus the Persian.

Bible crossword puzzle: The king's letter
ACROSS
4) living
5) trusted
6) prospered
8) bones

DOWN
1) den
2) wonders
3) destroyed
4) lions
6) peace
7) Darius

Comprehension worksheets: Babylon discovered?
1. Abraham and Balaam
2. Ask children to answer this question
3. Modern-day Iraq

Read and sequence worksheet: Daniel and the lions
1 = H, 2 = C, 3 = F, 4 = G, 5 = A, 6 = I, 7 = B, 8 = E, 9 = J, 10 = D

◇ DISCOVER MORE ACTIVITY BOOKS! ◇

Available for purchase at www.biblepathwayadventures.com

Made in the USA
Middletown, DE
11 April 2023

28667656R00046